OF INSECTS

Honey Bees

by Colleen Sexton

BELLWETHER MEDIA · MINNEAPOLIS, MN

BLASTOFF! READERS
2

Note to Librarians, Teachers, and Parents:

Blastoff! Readers are carefully developed by literacy experts and combine standards-based content with developmentally appropriate text.

Level 1 provides the most support through repetition of high-frequency words, light text, predictable sentence patterns, and strong visual support.

Level 2 offers early readers a bit more challenge through varied simple sentences, increased text load, and less repetition of high-frequency words.

Level 3 advances early-fluent readers toward fluency through increased text and concept load, less reliance on visuals, longer sentences, and more literary language.

Whichever book is right for your reader, Blastoff! Readers are the perfect books to build confidence and encourage a love of reading that will last a lifetime!

This edition first published in 2007 by Bellwether Media.

No part of this publication may be reproduced in whole or in part without written permission of the publisher. For information regarding permission, write to Bellwether Media Inc., Attention: Permissions Department, Post Office Box 1C, Minnetonka, MN 55345-9998.

Library of Congress Cataloging-in-Publication Data
Sexton, Colleen A.
  Honey bees / by Colleen Sexton.
    p. cm. — (World of insects)
Summary: "Simple text accompanied by full-color photographs give an upclose look at honey bees. Intended for kindergarten through third grade students"—Provided by publisher.
  Includes bibliographical references and index.
  ISBN-13: 978-1-60014-052-5 (hardcover : alk. paper)
  ISBN-10: 1-60014-052-1 (hardcover : alk. paper)
  1. Honeybee—Juvenile literature. I. Title.

QL568.A6S48 2007
595.79'9—dc22   2006034962

Contents

Honey bees are busy **insects**.

They work hard making
honey on summer days.

Honey bees have a yellow
body with black stripes.

Hair covers their body.

Honey bees have six legs.

Honey bees have four wings.

stinger

Honey bees have a **stinger**.
They may sting people, animals,
or other insects that bother them.

antennas

Honey bees have two **antennas**. They use antennas to smell things.

Honey bees gather **pollen** from flowers. This yellow dust sticks to the bee's body.

Honey bees carry lumps of pollen on their back legs.

Honey bees visit hundreds of flowers in a day. They carry pollen from flower to flower.

14

Flowers need honey bees to bring new pollen. They use this pollen to make seeds.

Honey bees also gather **nectar** from flowers.

tongue

They suck nectar through a long tongue that is like a straw.

Honey bees carry the nectar and pollen to their home.

18

Honey bees live in a **hive** with thousands of other bees.

The hive holds a wax **comb**. Honey bees fill holes in the comb with nectar.

The nectar dries and turns into honey. Honey is sweet to eat!

Glossary

antennas—the feelers on an insect's head; insects use their antennas to touch and smell things.

comb—a wax container with many holes; honey bees use the combs for raising young, storing food, and making honey.

hive—a home for honey bees; hives are made up of many combs.

insect—a small animal with six legs and a body divided into three parts; there are more insects in the world than any other kind of animal.

nectar—sweet juice that flowers make; honey bees drink nectar and make it into honey.

pollen—a dust that flowers use to make seeds; honey bees help flowers make seeds by moving pollen from flower to flower.

stinger—a sharp part on a honey bee's body that can pump poison; the bee stings to protect the hive.

To Learn More

AT THE LIBRARY

Cole, Joanna. *The Magic School Bus: Inside a Beehive*. New York: Scholastic, 1996.

Gibbons, Gail. *The Honey Makers*. New York: Morrow Junior Books, 1997.

Kalman, Bobbie. *The Life Cycle of a Honeybee*. New York: Crabtree Publishing, 2004.

Micucci, Charles. *The Life and Times of the Honeybee*. New York: Ticknor & Fields Books, 1995.

ON THE WEB

Learning more about honey bees is as easy as 1, 2, 3.

1. Go to www.factsurfer.com

2. Enter "honey bees" into search box.

3. Click the "Surf" button and you will see a list of related web sites.

With factsurfer.com, finding more information is just a click away.

Index

The photographs in this book are reproduced through the courtesy of: Chartchai Meesangnin, front cover; Nikolic Dejan, p. 4; Chepko Danil Vitalevich, p. 5; Van Truan, p. 6; Pot of Grass Productions, p. 7; Bob Jensen/Alamy, p. 8; alle, p. 9; Hans Pfletschinger/Getty Images, p. 10; ImageState/Alamy, p. 11; Juan Martinez, p. 12; blickwinkel/Alamy, p. 13; Kinlem, pp. 14, 20; WizData, Inc., p. 15; Phil Degginger/Alamy, p. 16; Hway Kiong Lim, p. 17; Steve McWilliam, p. 18; Steve Cukrov, p. 19; Darrin Jenkins/Alamy, p. 21.